Y0-BBX-184

OIL AND COAL

by Nikole Brooks Bethea

ENERGY LAB:
OIL AND COAL

CHERRY LAKE PUBLISHING • ANN ARBOR, MICHIGAN

CHERRY LAKE Publishing

Published in the United States of America
by Cherry Lake Publishing
Ann Arbor, Michigan
www.cherrylakepublishing.com

Printed in the United States of America
Corporate Graphics Inc.
January 2013
CLFA10

Consultants: Burtron H. Davis, Associate Director, Clean Fuels and Chemicals, Center for
Applied Energy Research, University of Kentucky; Marla Conn, reading/literacy specialist and
educational consultant

Editorial direction: Book design and illustration:
Lauren Coss   Emily Love

Photo credits: Leonid Ikan/Fotolia, cover, 1; Shutterstock Images, 5, 15; Karl Naundorf/
Fotolia, 6; Cheryl Casey/Shutterstock Images, 9; SuriyaPhoto/Shutterstock Images, 11;
Juan Camilo Bernal/Shutterstock Images, 13; Przemek Tokar/Shutterstock Images, 16;
V. J. Matthew/Shutterstock Images, 19; Vitoriano Jr./Shutterstock Images, 21; Mark Winfrey/
Shutterstock Images, 22; Zeljko Santrac/iStockphoto, 25; Christopher Futcher/iStockphoto, 27

Library of Congress Cataloging-in-Publication Data
Bethea, Nikole Brooks.
  Oil and coal / Nikole Brooks Bethea.
      pages cm. – (Energy lab)
  Includes index.
  ISBN 978-1-61080-897-2 (hardback : alk. paper) – ISBN 978-1-61080-922-1 (paperback : alk.
paper) – ISBN 978-1-61080-947-4 (ebook) – ISBN 978-1-61080-972-6 (hosted ebook)
  1. Petroleum–Juvenile literature. 2. Coal–Juvenile literature. I. Title.

TP355.B48 2013
553.2'8–dc23

                          2012032568

**Cherry Lake Publishing would like to acknowledge the work of The Partnership for
21st Century Skills. Please visit www.21stCenturySkills.org for more information.**

TABLE OF CONTENTS

You are being given a mission. The facts in What You Know will help you accomplish it. Remember the clues from What You Know while you are reading the story. The clues and the story will help you answer the questions at the end of the book. Have fun on this adventure!

Your mission is to investigate how oil and coal are used as energy sources. Right now, **fossil fuels**, including oil and coal, provide more than 80 percent of the energy used in the United States. People use oil and coal every day to fuel cars and buses, create electricity, and more. Oil and coal supplies are limited. But they still have an important role to play in our energy future. You need to learn more about these important fuels to understand why. How were they formed? How do they produce energy? What effects do oil and coal have on the environment? Review the facts in What You Know to help you with your mission.

WHAT YOU KNOW

★ Fossil fuels include coal, oil, and natural gas.
★ Fossil fuels are the remains of plants and animals that died millions of years ago.
★ Coal is a black or brown rock made up mostly of **carbon**. Most coal in the United States is used to generate electricity.

Gasoline produced from oil is an important energy source that helps power our cars.

★ Crude oil, or **petroleum**, is a liquid fossil fuel. Petroleum is our primary source of energy for transportation.

★ Fossil fuels take millions of years to form. They cannot form as fast as we are using them. This makes them nonrenewable energy sources.

Abby Parks is doing a science project on how energy is used today. She will meet with experts to learn about oil and coal. Carry out your mission by reading Abby's journal.

I decide to kick off my research by learning more about oil. I know North Dakota is known for producing a lot of oil. So I make a trip to a North Dakota oil field to start my research. Penny Dorn is the vice president of the oil company.

The oil pumped by wells comes from small creatures that turned into fossil fuels after millions of years of heat and pressure.

"Welcome to our oil field, Abby!" she says. "Before I show you around, how about a little bit of background on oil?"

Penny explains that oil is a fossil fuel. It formed from tiny sea creatures that lived more than 300 million years ago. These sea creatures sank to the bottom of ancient oceans when they died. Then they were covered with layers of mud. The layers became thicker until there were hundreds and sometimes thousands of feet of earth covering the dead sea life. Over millions of years, pressure and heat turned the sea life fossils into oil and natural gas.

Penny also tells me that oil wells have been around for a while. In Titusville, Pennsylvania, Edwin L. Drake drilled the first oil well in 1859. People began using oil to produce gasoline. In the 1880s, the demand for gasoline increased because cars started being produced. By the 1920s, there were 9 million cars in the United States. Gas stations began popping up everywhere. Since that time, we have become dependent on crude oil.

Next, I learn that the oil well pumps oil from a reservoir underground. "Do you know what an oil reservoir is?" she asks. I imagine that it's an underground pool of oil. But Penny says oil reservoirs are actually areas of rock. These spots have droplets of oil stored in the **pores**, or spaces, of the rocks.

UNDERWATER OIL

Not all oil is located underneath land. A lot of oil can be found beneath the world's oceans. To get at this oil, companies need to drill deep into the sea floor. But many people have concerns about this kind of offshore drilling. On April 20, 2010, the *Deepwater Horizon* offshore oil rig exploded. The rig was drilling a well in the Gulf of Mexico about 40 miles (65 km) southeast of Louisiana. Oil spilled for almost three months. The well was finally capped on July 12, 2010, stopping the flow of oil. The spill caused a lot of damage to the environment. It also made many people question the use of offshore drilling.

Drilling for oil is expensive. Scientists use sound waves to determine the best places to drill for oil. Sound travels through different types of rocks at different speeds. Computers help measure how fast sound waves move through rock.

"Once we have found an oil reservoir," Penny says, "we drill a production well. As soon as the well hits the reservoir, oil often rises. As the pressure in an oil well goes down, the oil will no longer rise on its own." Penny tells me

Workers clean up a Florida beach after the 2010 Gulf of Mexico oil spill.

that they install pumps at this point. The pumps remove the oil from the ground.

I look at the many pumps around us. I know that this oil could eventually become the gasoline that powers my dad's car. But I wonder how it becomes gasoline. ★

Now I know how oil is taken from deep within the earth. But I want to know more about how this oil is turned into the fuel that powers our cars and buses. Today I am visiting an oil **refinery** in Minnesota. The refinery is gigantic. There are pipes, tanks, towers, and stacks as far as I can see. I notice something else about the refinery. It smells a little like rotten eggs.

"What's that smell?" I ask Brett Bakkus. Brett is an engineer who works at the refinery. He has offered to show me around.

"Crude oil has a lot of different chemicals," Brett explains. "These need to be removed before the oil can become something useful, like gasoline. The odor you're noticing is the smell of these chemicals being released into the atmosphere. These chemicals won't harm you in small amounts," he says. "But refineries still have to be careful. If a leak or a spill happens, some of these chemicals can get into the water. This can be harmful to people and wildlife."

Brett continues, "Crude oil is not very useful when it first comes out of the ground. It is made of many different hydrocarbons. These are chains of carbon and hydrogen atoms. The purpose of the refinery is to separate crude oil

At oil refineries, crude oil from the ground is made into the gasoline that powers our cars.

into its different parts. Each part forms a different product and has different properties."

Brett explains that the first process at the refinery is this separation. Each of the hydrocarbons in the crude oil turns from liquid to gas at a different temperature. This allows the parts that make up the crude oil to separate.

After each of the parts has been separated from the crude oil, refineries must remove the impurities from them. Next, the different parts are mixed to create the desired products. Pipelines carry the finished product, including gasoline, from the refinery to storage areas. Delivery trucks bring the products to gas stations and other places that use them.

"The refinement process has improved a lot," Brett says. "A hundred years ago, only a small part of the oil could be used for transportation fuel. Today, almost all of the oil can be used. Fuel and vehicles have both improved. These improvements allow us to travel about twice as far on a gallon of fuel as we could in 1960."

Brett tells me that oil can have some negative effects. Burning gasoline releases carbon dioxide and other **greenhouse gases** into the atmosphere. Most scientists

ELECTRIC CARS

Vehicles that run on gasoline only use about 20 percent of the energy stored in gasoline to drive. Electric vehicles can use about 60 percent of the energy for driving power. Hybrid and all-electric vehicles help us use oil and coal in ways that are better for the environment. Hybrid vehicles use two power sources, usually gas and electricity. All-electric vehicles don't give off pollution. However, the power plant that generated the electricity usually gives off some pollution.

Electric cars use gasoline more efficiently than gasoline-only cars.

believe these gases are contributing to a gradual warming of the earth's average temperature. Because of this, many people think we should cut down on our oil use. We should try to find ways to use oil even more efficiently.

I guess oil has its advantages and disadvantages like any energy source. I thank Brett for showing me around. On to my next destination! ★

After spending time studying oil, it's time to switch gears to focus on another fossil fuel: coal. Today I am visiting an underground coal mine in Ohio. When I get there, Eileen Kirkpatrick takes me right to an elevator. She is the mine superintendent. As we ride deep into the ground, Eileen tells me more about coal.

She tells me coal actually formed in a way that is very similar to the way oil formed. Coal formed from plants that lived in swampy areas over 300 million years ago. After the plants died, they were covered with more plants, soil, and water. The plants turned to peat, an **organic** sediment made up of decayed stems, roots, bark, and twigs. Over time, the pressure from the upper layers squeezed water from the peat. Heat from within the earth caused the peat to break down. Gases were forced out. And the peat changed to coal.

"Have you ever been to a coal mine before?" Eileen asks. I shake my head. "Well, coal has been around a long time. For thousands of years, humans have used it as a fuel source for heating their homes. In the 1800s, the Industrial Revolution took place in England and other parts of the world. People made huge improvements in technology during this time. Much of this new technology relied on coal

Over hundreds of millions of years, heat and pressure turned ancient plants into coal.

as a fuel. This increased coal's role as an energy source. Steamboats and locomotives became important forms of transportation. Coal fueled their boilers."

The elevator finally stops. Eileen says we have reached the coal seam. The coal seam is a layer of coal between layers of rock. I see a large machine cutting coal from the seam. "This machine is called a continuous miner," Eileen explains.

On the front of the continuous miner I see rows of teeth. The machine rotates quickly, allowing the teeth to scrape coal from the seam. The continuous miner scoops the mined coal and moves it to the back of the machine. Conveyor belts move the coal up to the surface of the mine. Then it will be processed.

Eileen points to the columns standing throughout the underground mine. "These are pillars," she says. "In this mine, we use a mining process known as room and pillar mining. The continuous miner cuts rooms into the coal deposit, leaving the pillars. The pillars support the roof and keep the mine from collapsing on us."

The continuous miner helps us mine coal with less danger to human lives.

RISKY MINING

Coal mines are built with special safety precautions. But coal mining can still be very dangerous. In the past, mines weren't nearly as safe as they are today. Occasionally the mines caved in. Sometimes this killed everyone inside. Other times, buildups of gas below the ground led to explosions. Even though mines are much safer today, mining accidents can still happen.

We ride back up in the elevator. Once we reach the surface, Eileen suggests we look at how the coal is processed and transported. We walk over to the processing plant. Here coal is crushed, sorted, and washed. This removes a lot of the rock and dirt that can't be burned as fuel. I hear a train pulling up. Almost 100 empty railcars are waiting to be loaded. Eileen tells me this trainload of coal is being shipped to a utilities company. The coal will be burned to generate electricity at a power plant. Power plants use a lot of coal. Some bigger plants use an entire trainload of coal almost every day. That's a lot of coal! I decide to visit a power plant next to see exactly how a plant turns this coal into energy. ★

For my next stop, I'm visiting a coal-fired power plant in Mississippi. I want to find out how coal is used to make electricity. Ben Cosas meets me as soon as I arrive. Ben is the plant manager. He hands me a small container that holds a bit of the coal his plant uses. This coal isn't shaped like the rocks I saw at the coal mine. Instead, it has been crushed and ground into a fine black powder.

"A power plant has a lot of moving parts," Ben explains. "We feed this coal into a firebox where it mixes with air and burns. The firebox provides heat to a big boiler. We pump water through pipes inside the boiler. As the coal burns in the firebox, it heats the water inside these pipes. Once the water becomes hot enough to boil, it changes into steam. The steam is piped to a **turbine**, a machine with large blades. The pressure of the moving steam turns the blades in the turbine. As these blades turn, they spin the turbine shaft."

Ben tells me that the turbine shaft is connected to a **generator**. As the shaft turns, the generator produces electricity.

After completing its work in the turbine, the steam is sent into a condenser. The condenser is a large chamber

Approximately half of the electricity used in the United States is produced by coal-fired power plants.

with tubes of cool water running through it. The steam condenses on the tubes, changing back into water. The water can then be reused in the boiler.

"Large amounts of water are required for this cooling process," Ben adds. "That's why this power plant is next to a river. The hot water from the tubes is then sent to the cooling towers."

He grins. "Coal-fired power plants are great because they are more efficient than many other energy sources, such as solar power. They are also pretty cheap to operate," he explains. "Plus, even though coal is a nonrenewable resource, we have a lot of it. And much of it can be mined and sold right here in the United States. That's good for our economy!"

He adds, "But as with all energy sources, there are some downsides. For one, coal-fired power plants release a lot of carbon dioxide gas." I remember what I learned about greenhouse gases at the oil refinery. Ben tells me coal-fired power plants also contribute to this trapping of gases, called the greenhouse effect.

"Even though coal power is more efficient than many other energy sources, most older coal plants are only about

THE GREENHOUSE EFFECT

Earth only absorbs some of the sun's energy. The other energy is reflected to space. A natural layer of gases in the atmosphere traps some of the sun's heat, warming the earth. This is called the greenhouse effect. Without the greenhouse effect, the earth would be much colder and covered in ice. However, humans are adding greenhouse gases to the atmosphere. Burning fossil fuels is a major source of additional greenhouse gases. Most scientists believe these added gases trap more heat on the earth, increasing the earth's average temperature. This is known as global warming, or climate change.

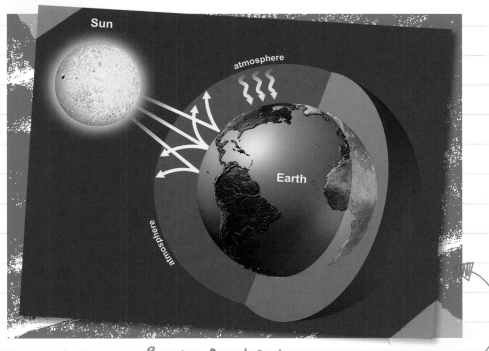

Burning fossil fuels, such as coal, contributes to the greenhouse effect.

30 percent efficient," Ben says. "Think about it this way. If you were doing your math homework at 100 percent efficiency, it would take you one hour. If you were doing your homework at 1 percent efficiency, it would take you 100 hours. New technology can help make plants more efficient," he adds. "But updating older plants to the new technology will be expensive."

My trip to the power plant has given me a lot to think about. Ben said there is technology that can make a coal-fired power plant more environmentally friendly. I decide to investigate further. ★

October 30:
CLEANER COAL?

I've learned a lot about some of the pros and cons of coal power. Now I want to learn more about the ways to control the air pollution created by burning coal in power plants.

Today I'm visiting a coal-fired power plant in Maine. This plant has recently built a new **scrubber**. A scrubber is a device that removes pollutants from the gases created by a coal-fired power plant. When I arrive, the power plant's

Some power plants have scrubbers. These tall towers help a coal-fired power plant reduce its air pollution.

environmental engineer Terry Schneider greets me. I tell Terry about my trip to the Mississippi power plant and what I learned about carbon dioxide.

"So you know a thing or two about greenhouse gases!" Terry says. "Carbon dioxide is one of the downsides to coal power. But it is not the only pollutant released when coal is turned into energy."

He explains that sulfur is a yellow substance found naturally in coal. Some of this sulfur was in the ancient plant life from which the coal formed. Other sulfur came from ancient seawater that had contact with the coal as it was forming. As coal burns, the sulfur combines with oxygen. This forms sulfur dioxide, a poisonous gas that can be bad for the environment.

Clean air rules limit the amount of sulfur dioxide power plants can release when they burn coal. All power plants built after 1978 must include a sulfur-removal system if they are burning coal with a lot of sulfur. One way to remove sulfur is to simply crush the coal and wash it before burning it.

During **combustion**, the stage where the coal is burned, smoke is created. The smoke then passes through the tower-shaped scrubber. The scrubber removes sulfur from the smoke before it is released into the air.

CARBON CAPTURE PLANTS

Most power plants burn fossil fuels. This releases large amounts of carbon dioxide into the atmosphere, which can lead to global warming. Carbon capture is a new technology that traps the carbon dioxide before it is released into the atmosphere. First the carbon dioxide is captured. Then it is piped deep underground. There, it is permanently stored in rock formations that are often more than a half mile (.8 km) underground. The site is watched to make sure the carbon dioxide doesn't escape back to the surface.

Terry says it's still impossible to make coal completely pollution-free. The scrubbers help remove most of the pollutants. But they can't get them all out. Small amounts of sulfur dioxide and other pollutants still make their way into the atmosphere and the environment.

"Researchers and engineers are working hard to make coal power cleaner and more efficient," Terry says. "Fossil fuels are an important part of meeting our energy needs. But eventually they will run out. It is important for us to protect our resources and make the most of them. We also

You can do your part to protect our fossil fuel supply by turning off the lights in an empty room.

need to protect our environment by finding ways to use coal energy responsibly."

I thank Terry for showing me around. I can't believe how much I've learned about oil and coal! ★

You did it! You learned how coal and oil originally formed. You've studied how they are removed from the ground. You also learned that fossil fuels can be burned to provide heat. This heat can provide transportation energy. Or it can power a turbine to produce electricity. You also discovered how a refinery creates different petroleum products. You saw how the production of electricity causes air pollution. But you also learned about modern methods to prevent fossil fuels from polluting the environment as much. Congratulations on completing your mission!

CONSIDER THIS

★ Explain how coal and oil formed.

★ Why are coal and oil considered nonrenewable energy sources?

★ Explain how oil is found and then recovered from an oil well.

Fossil fuels help us get from place to place.
How does your family use fossil fuels?

★ How do power plants turn coal into electricity?
★ What are ways to reduce pollution from the coal used to generate electricity?

GLOSSARY

carbon (KAHR-buhn) an element in living things that can trigger climate change in excess amounts

combustion (kuhm-BUS-chuhn) the process of burning

fossil fuel (FAH-suhl fyoo-uhl) coal, oil, or natural gas formed from ancient plants and animals

generator (JEN-uh-ray-tur) a machine that produces electricity

greenhouse gas (GREEN-hous gas) gases that trap heat in the atmosphere

organic (or-GAN-ik) material from living things

petroleum (puh-TROH-lee-uhm) a thick liquid found underground that can be used to make gasoline

pore (POR) an open space in a rock that can contain air, water, or petroleum

refinery (ri-FYE-nur-ee) a factory that processes crude oil into a final product, such as gasoline

scrubber (SKRUH-bur) a device that removes pollutants at a coal-fired power plant

turbine (TUR-buhn) a machine that spins an electric generator

LEARN MORE

BOOKS

Bedford, Kate. *Coal*. North Mankato, MN: Stargazer Books, 2007.

Morgan, Sally. *The Pros and Cons of Oil, Gas, and Coal*. New York: Rosen, 2008.

Solway, Andrew. *Fossil Fuels*. Pleasantville, NY: Gareth Stevens, 2008.

WEB SITES

Adventures in Energy

http://www.adventuresinenergy.org

Research the processes involved in getting oil and natural gas from the well to the American consumer.

Energy Kids

http://www.eia.gov/kids

Follow the energy links for information on different energy sources and their histories, including energy-related games and activities.

Fossil Fuel Energy

http://www.kidzworld.com/article/1423-fossil-fuel-energy

Learn more about fossil fuels, including how we get them and how we use them.

HELP CONSERVE FOSSIL FUELS

Fossil fuels are a nonrenewable resource. But you can conserve fossil fuels by reducing the amount of electricity and petroleum products you use. Turn off lights and televisions when you are not using them. Don't leave doors open for air-conditioning or heat to escape. Even recycling aluminum cans saves energy. Look around your home and make a list of ways you can help conserve fossil fuels. Follow this list for a week. Take notes on which of these ways are easy to adapt to and which are hard.

SHRINK YOUR CARBON USE

The amount of greenhouse gases you produce is sometimes called your carbon footprint. Visit an online carbon footprint calculator to estimate how much carbon dioxide your household produces in a year. Examine your results—where can you reduce emissions? Can you turn off the lights every time you leave a room? Can you replace outdoor electrical lighting with solar-powered lamps? What about growing your own food to reduce driving trips to the grocery store? What are other things you could do to reduce emissions?

INDEX

Nikole Brooks Bethea is a licensed professional engineer. She holds bachelor's and master's degrees in environmental engineering from the University of Florida. She is the author of both nonfiction and fiction books for children. She lives in the Florida Panhandle with her husband and four sons.

ABOUT THE CONSULTANTS

Burt Davis studies methods to convert coal to transportation fuels using the Fischer-Tropsch process. First coal is gasified to carbon monoxide and hydrogen, a synthesis gas. A catalyst, or substance that helps a chemical reaction occur, is used to convert the synthesis gas to liquid and wax hydrocarbons. These are further refined to produce gasoline and diesel fuels.

Marla Conn is a reading/literacy specialist and an educational consultant. Her specialized consulting work consists of assigning guided reading levels to trade books, writing and developing user guides and lesson plans, and correlating books to curriculum and national standards.